"Checking In: The Ultimate Guide to the Hotel Industry"
Introduction

Welcome to "Checking In: The Ultimate Guide to the Hotel Industry". This book is designed to provide a comprehensive overview of the hotel industry, from its history and evolution to current trends and best practices.

The hotel industry has been an integral part of human civilization for centuries, with the first recorded lodging establishments dating back to ancient times. Since then, the industry has grown and evolved to meet the changing needs and preferences of travelers, becoming an important economic contributor in many countries.

In recent years, the hotel industry has undergone significant transformations driven by advancements in technology, changing consumer behavior, and global events such as the COVID-19 pandemic. These changes have presented both challenges and opportunities for hotel operators, making it more important than ever to stay informed and adapt to new trends and developments.

This book is divided into several sections, each focusing on different aspects of the hotel industry. The first section covers the history and evolution of lodging, from the earliest inns and taverns to the modern hotel chains and boutique hotels of today. The second section explores the different types of hotels and their unique characteristics, such as luxury hotels, budget hotels, and resort hotels.

The third section delves into the operations and management of hotels, including topics such as revenue management, marketing and branding, and customer service. The fourth section looks at current trends and challenges facing the industry, including sustainability, technology, and the impact of the COVID-19 pandemic.

Throughout the book, we will also feature case studies and interviews with industry experts, providing real-world examples and insights into the hotel industry. Whether you are a hotel manager, aspiring hotelier, or simply interested in learning more about the world of hospitality, this book will serve as a valuable resource and guide.

We hope that this book will inspire you to appreciate the rich history and complexity of the hotel industry, and equip you with the knowledge and skills to succeed in this exciting and dynamic field. So, let's begin our journey of discovery and exploration into the world of hotels!

INDEX

Section 1: History and Evolution of Lodging

- # Chapter 1: The Origins of Lodging

The history of lodging can be traced back to ancient times, when travelers would seek shelter in temples, palaces, and other public buildings. In medieval Europe, inns and taverns began to emerge as a popular form of lodging, providing travelers with a place to rest, eat, and drink. In the 18th century, the concept of the modern hotel began to take shape, with the opening of the City Hotel in New York City in 1794.

The City Hotel was the first hotel in America to offer private rooms with locks and keys, as well as a public dining room and a separate bar. This marked a significant departure from the traditional inn or tavern, which provided a communal space for sleeping, eating, and socializing. The success of the City Hotel inspired other entrepreneurs to open similar establishments, and the modern hotel industry was born.

During the 19th century, hotels began to grow in size and sophistication, with the opening of grand hotels like the Ritz in London and the Waldorf Astoria in New York City. These hotels were characterized by their luxurious amenities, including fine dining restaurants, ballrooms, and private suites. They also attracted wealthy travelers from around the world, who sought out the prestige and exclusivity that these hotels offered.

In the early 20th century, the hotel industry began to consolidate, with the formation of hotel chains and franchises. These chains allowed hotels to share branding, marketing, and operational resources, while still maintaining their individual identities. The first hotel chain was the Quality Courts United, which was founded in 1939 and later became the Holiday Inn chain.

In the 1960s and 1970s, the concept of the boutique hotel began to emerge, offering travelers a more personalized and intimate experience. Boutique hotels were characterized by their unique design, decor, and amenities, as well as their emphasis on personalized service and attention to detail.

Today, the hotel industry continues to evolve, with new types of lodging emerging to meet the changing needs and preferences of travelers. One of the most significant developments in recent years has been the rise of alternative lodging options like vacation rentals, home-sharing platforms like Airbnb, and hostels. These alternatives have disrupted the traditional hotel industry, offering travelers more affordable, flexible, and authentic experiences.

In response, many hotels have sought to differentiate themselves by offering unique amenities and experiences, such as wellness programs, cultural activities, and local cuisine. They have also invested heavily in technology, from mobile apps and online booking platforms to artificial intelligence and virtual reality.

Another major trend in the hotel industry is sustainability. As travelers become more conscious of their impact on the environment, hotels are seeking to reduce their carbon footprint and promote responsible tourism. This has led to the development of eco-friendly hotels, which use renewable energy sources, conserve water, and minimize waste.

In summary, the history and evolution of lodging have been shaped by the changing needs and preferences of travelers, as well as by advances in technology, marketing, and management. From the earliest inns and taverns to the grand hotels of the 19th and 20th centuries, and from the rise of hotel chains and franchises to the emergence of boutique hotels and alternative lodging options, the hotel industry has always been at the forefront of innovation and change. Today, as the industry faces new challenges and opportunities, it continues to adapt and evolve, offering travelers a range of options and experiences that are tailored to their individual needs and preferences.

The origins of lodging can be traced back to ancient times when people would travel and seek shelter in temples, palaces, and other public buildings. However, the concept of commercial lodging did not emerge until the Middle Ages when inns and taverns began to appear in Europe.

These inns provided travelers with a place to rest, eat, and drink, and were often owned by local residents who would offer up their own homes as lodging for travelers. Inns typically offered a communal sleeping area, while taverns focused more on drinking and socializing. Over time, these establishments began to develop more formalized systems for lodging, with separate rooms and more comfortable amenities.

In the 18th century, the modern hotel industry began to take shape with the opening of the City Hotel in New York City in 1794. The City Hotel was the first hotel in America to offer private rooms with locks and keys, as well as a public dining room and a separate bar. This marked a significant departure from the traditional inn or tavern, which provided a communal space for sleeping, eating, and socializing. The success of the City Hotel inspired other entrepreneurs to open similar establishments, and the modern hotel industry was born.

In the early days of the hotel industry, most hotels were small and locally owned, with a focus on providing basic amenities like a bed and a meal. However, as travel became more common and the middle class began to emerge, the demand for more luxurious accommodations increased. This led to the rise of grand hotels, which were characterized by their opulent decor, fine dining restaurants, and exclusive clientele.

One of the earliest examples of a grand hotel was the Tremont House in Boston, which opened in 1829. The Tremont House was the first hotel to offer indoor plumbing, as well as the first to provide separate bathrooms for men and women. It also had a dining room that could seat up to 600 guests, making it a popular destination for high society events.

During the late 19th and early 20th centuries, the hotel industry continued to grow and evolve. Many grand hotels were built in major cities around the world, including the Ritz in London, the Savoy in New York City, and the Carlton in Cannes. These hotels were known for their luxurious amenities and exclusive clientele, and they helped to establish the hotel industry as a symbol of wealth and status.

In the mid-20th century, the hotel industry began to consolidate, with the formation of hotel chains and franchises. These chains allowed hotels to share branding, marketing, and operational resources, while still maintaining their individual identities. The first hotel chain was the Quality Courts United, which was founded in 1939 and later became the Holiday Inn chain.

Today, the hotel industry continues to evolve, with new types of lodging emerging to meet the changing needs and preferences of travelers. One of the most significant developments in recent years has been the rise of alternative lodging options like vacation rentals, home-sharing platforms like Airbnb, and hostels. These alternatives have disrupted the traditional hotel industry, offering travelers more affordable, flexible, and authentic experiences.

In response, many hotels have sought to differentiate themselves by offering unique amenities and experiences, such as wellness programs, cultural activities, and local cuisine. They have also invested heavily in technology, from mobile apps and online booking platforms to artificial intelligence and virtual reality.

Another major trend in the hotel industry is sustainability. As travelers become more conscious of their impact on the environment, hotels are seeking to reduce their carbon footprint and promote responsible tourism. This has led to the development of eco-friendly hotels, which use renewable energy sources, conserve water, and minimize waste.

In summary, the origins of lodging can be traced back to ancient times, but the modern hotel industry did not emerge until the 18th century.

• **Chapter 2: Inns and Taverns**

Inns and taverns were among the earliest forms of lodging and socializing establishments in Europe. They provided a space for travellers to rest, eat, and drink, and were often owned by local residents who would offer up their own homes as lodging for travellers.

Inns typically offered a communal sleeping area, while taverns focused more on drinking and socializing. The earliest inns were likely established during the Roman Empire, but the concept really took off in medieval Europe with the rise of long-distance trade and pilgrimage.

Inns and taverns were typically located along major trade routes or near popular pilgrimage sites, and provided a vital service to travellers who needed a safe and comfortable place to rest and recover before continuing their journey.

Inns were often identified by signs that hung outside the establishment, and each sign had a specific meaning or association. For example, the sign of a lion might indicate that the inn was owned by a member of the nobility, while the sign of a swan might indicate that the inn had a nearby river or lake.

Taverns, on the other hand, were typically associated with drinking and socializing. They were often located in urban areas and served as a gathering place for locals and travellers alike. Taverns might offer food and lodging as well, but their primary function was to provide a space for people to gather and socialize.

Inns and taverns were often regulated by local authorities, who would set standards for cleanliness, safety, and pricing. Some inns and taverns were more reputable than others, and travellers had to be careful to avoid establishments that were unsafe or dishonest.

Over time, inns and taverns began to develop more formalized systems for lodging, with separate rooms and more comfortable amenities. This trend continued into the 18th and 19th centuries with the rise of the modern hotel industry, which offered private rooms with locks and keys, as well as more luxurious accommodations.

Despite the rise of the hotel industry, inns and taverns continue to play an important role in the hospitality industry today. Many inns and taverns have been refurbished and updated to offer modern amenities while still retaining their historic charm.

In conclusion, inns and taverns were among the earliest forms of lodging and socializing establishments in Europe, and played a vital role in supporting long-distance trade and pilgrimage. While the concept has evolved over time with the rise of the hotel industry, inns and taverns continue to be an important part of the hospitality industry today.

• Chapter 3: The Birth of the Modern Hotel

The birth of the modern hotel can be traced back to the early 19th century, when industrialization and increased mobility created a demand for new forms of lodging. The first modern hotels were built in major urban centers, such as London and Paris, to cater to the needs of wealthy travelers and businesspeople.

The first modern hotel is often considered to be the Tremont House in Boston, which opened in 1829. The Tremont House was notable for its luxurious amenities, including private rooms with locks and keys, indoor plumbing, and even an elevator. It quickly became a model for other hotels around the world.

One of the key innovations of the modern hotel was the concept of the hotel restaurant. The Tremont House featured a restaurant that offered a menu of high-quality food and drink, as well as a separate dining room for women. This was a significant departure from the earlier inns and taverns, which typically provided communal dining areas.

Another important feature of the modern hotel was the use of technology to improve efficiency and comfort. The Tremont House was one of the first hotels to use steam-powered elevators, which allowed guests to easily access the upper floors of the building. Other hotels soon followed suit, using technology to improve everything from heating and ventilation to communication and transportation.

The rise of the modern hotel coincided with the growth of the tourism industry. As more people began to travel for leisure, hotels became an important part of the travel experience. Hotels were no longer just a place to sleep and eat, but also a destination in their own right. This led to the development of a new type of hotel, the resort hotel, which focused on providing leisure activities and entertainment for guests.

As the hotel industry continued to grow and evolve, new trends and innovations emerged. One of the most significant was the development of the chain hotel, which allowed hotels to offer consistent service and amenities across multiple locations. The first chain hotel was the Great Western Hotel, which opened in 1838 and eventually grew to become the largest hotel chain in the world.

Today, the hotel industry is a global phenomenon, with hotels and resorts located in every corner of the world. While the concept of the modern hotel has continued to evolve over time, the basic principles of comfort, convenience, and hospitality remain the same. From budget hotels to luxury resorts, the hotel industry continues to play an important role in the global economy and the travel industry.

In conclusion, the birth of the modern hotel in the early 19th century represented a significant departure from earlier forms of lodging such as inns and taverns. With its focus on luxury amenities, technology, and efficient service, the modern hotel quickly became an important part of the travel industry. Today, the hotel industry continues to evolve and innovate, while still retaining the basic principles of comfort and hospitality that have made it a global phenomenon.

· **Chapter 4: Hotel Chains and Franchises**

Hotel chains and franchises are an important part of the hospitality industry, offering consistent service and amenities across multiple locations. A hotel chain is a group of hotels that are owned and operated by the same company, while a franchise is a hotel that is independently owned but operates under the branding and standards of a larger hotel company.

The concept of hotel chains and franchises dates back to the early 20th century, when hotels began to expand beyond their original locations. One of the first hotel chains was the Sheraton Hotel Company, which was founded in 1937 and quickly grew to become one of the largest hotel chains in the world.

Today, there are a wide variety of hotel chains and franchises operating around the world, catering to different types of travelers and budgets. Some of the most well-known hotel chains include Marriott, Hilton, and InterContinental Hotels Group (IHG).

Hotel chains and franchises offer a number of benefits for both guests and hotel owners. For guests, they provide a consistent level of service and amenities, regardless of the location. This can be particularly helpful for business travelers or frequent travelers who prefer to stay with a familiar brand.

For hotel owners, joining a hotel chain or franchise can provide access to a larger customer base and marketing support. It can also help them to streamline operations and improve efficiency, since they can take advantage of the systems and procedures developed by the larger hotel company.

In addition to hotel chains and franchises, there are also a number of other types of hotel affiliations and partnerships. These include soft brands, which are independent hotels that operate under a larger brand umbrella while retaining their unique character and identity. There are also hotel consortia, which are groups of independent hotels that band together for marketing and other purposes.

One of the key trends in the hotel industry in recent years has been the growth of boutique and lifestyle hotels, which offer a unique and personalized experience for guests. Many of these hotels are independent or part of smaller hotel groups, and they often prioritize design, local culture, and unique amenities over the standardization and consistency offered by larger hotel chains.

In conclusion, hotel chains and franchises are an important part of the hospitality industry, offering consistent service and amenities across multiple locations. They provide a number of benefits for both guests and hotel owners, and have been a key driver of the growth and expansion of the hotel industry over the past century. As the industry continues to evolve, we can expect to see new types of hotel affiliations and partnerships emerge, along with new trends in design and guest experience.

• Chapter 5: Boutique Hotels and Alternative Lodging

Boutique hotels and alternative lodging are a growing trend in the hospitality industry, offering unique and personalized experiences for travelers looking for something different from traditional hotels. Boutique hotels are typically small, independently owned hotels that prioritize design, individuality, and personal service, while alternative lodging includes a wide variety of accommodations such as vacation rentals, homestays, and hostels.

The concept of boutique hotels originated in the 1980s in major cities such as New York and London, where developers began to convert historic buildings and industrial spaces into small, stylish hotels. Today, boutique hotels can be found in cities and destinations around the world, and often cater to specific niches such as luxury travelers, foodies, or wellness enthusiasts.

Boutique hotels are known for their unique design and décor, which often incorporates local art and culture. They also tend to offer personalized service, with staff members who are knowledgeable about the local area and can make personalized recommendations for activities, dining, and sightseeing.

Alternative lodging, on the other hand, encompasses a wide range of accommodations that fall outside of the traditional hotel model. This includes vacation rentals such as Airbnb, which allow travelers to stay in someone's home or apartment, as well as hostels, which offer budget-friendly accommodations in shared dormitory-style rooms. Other types of alternative lodging include glamping, which combines the experience of camping with luxurious amenities, and farm stays, which allow guests to experience life on a working farm.

One of the key drivers of the growth of boutique hotels and alternative lodging is the changing preferences of travelers, particularly younger generations such as millennials and Gen Z. These travelers are looking for experiences that are unique, authentic, and personalized, and are less concerned with the standardization and consistency offered by traditional hotel chains.

Boutique hotels and alternative lodging also offer benefits for hotel owners, who can often operate with lower overhead costs and greater flexibility than traditional hotels. For example, a boutique hotel owner may be able to offer a more unique and personalized experience with a smaller staff, while an Airbnb host can supplement their income by renting out a spare room or vacation property.

In conclusion, boutique hotels and alternative lodging are a growing trend in the hospitality industry, offering unique and personalized experiences for travelers looking for something different from traditional hotels. They are driven by changing preferences among travelers, particularly younger generations, and offer benefits for both guests and hotel owners. As the industry continues to evolve, we can expect to see new types of alternative lodging emerge, as well as new trends in design and guest experience.

Section 2: Types of Hotels

There are many different types of hotels that cater to a wide range of travelers and their needs. Some hotels specialize in luxury and high-end amenities, while others offer more budget-friendly options for travelers on a tight budget. Here are some of the most common types of hotels:

1. Luxury Hotels: These hotels are typically located in prime locations and offer the highest level of amenities and service. They often feature high-end restaurants, spas, and other luxurious amenities. Some of the most well-known luxury hotel brands include Four Seasons, Ritz-Carlton, and Mandarin Oriental.

2. Boutique Hotels: These small, independently-owned hotels prioritize design, individuality, and personal service. They often feature unique décor and offer personalized recommendations for dining and sightseeing. Boutique hotels can

range from budget-friendly to high-end luxury properties.

3. Resort Hotels: These hotels are typically located in vacation destinations and offer a wide range of activities and amenities, such as pools, beaches, golf courses, and spa services. They often cater to families and offer a variety of children's programs and activities.

4. Bed and Breakfasts: These small, often family-owned properties offer a more homey, personalized experience than traditional hotels. They typically include breakfast in the room rate and may have shared common areas for guests.

5. Budget Hotels: These hotels offer basic accommodations and amenities at a lower price point than luxury or boutique hotels. They may be located in less desirable areas or have more basic amenities, but can be a good option for travelers on a tight budget.

6. Extended-Stay Hotels: These hotels are designed for travelers who are staying in one location for an extended period of time, such as for business or relocation. They typically offer larger rooms or suites with kitchenettes or full kitchens, as

well as laundry facilities and other amenities that make long-term stays more comfortable.

7. Casino Hotels: These hotels are typically located in major gambling destinations and offer on-site casinos and other entertainment options. They often feature high-end restaurants and luxury amenities.

8. Eco-Friendly Hotels: These hotels prioritize sustainability and minimizing their impact on the environment. They may use renewable energy sources, have water conservation measures in place, and use locally-sourced or organic products.

9. All-Inclusive Hotels: These hotels offer a comprehensive vacation experience, with all meals, drinks, and activities included in the room rate. They can be a good option for travelers who want to budget their expenses upfront and not worry about additional costs during their stay.

10. Historic Hotels: These hotels are typically housed in historic buildings or properties that have been restored or preserved for their cultural significance. They may offer guided tours or other historical activities for guests.

In conclusion, there are many different types of hotels that cater to a wide range of travelers and their needs. From luxury and boutique hotels to budget-friendly options and extended-stay properties, there is something for everyone. Each type of hotel offers its own unique amenities and experiences, and travelers should choose the type of hotel that best fits their budget and travel style.

• Chapter 6: Luxury Hotels

Luxury hotels are often considered the pinnacle of the hospitality industry, offering guests the highest level of service, amenities, and accommodations. These hotels are typically located in prime locations and cater to travelers who are seeking the best of the best when it comes to their lodging experience. In this article, we will explore the various aspects that make luxury hotels unique and desirable.

Location and Design

Luxury hotels are often located in prime locations, such as in the heart of a city or in a scenic natural setting. These hotels are typically situated near major tourist attractions or in areas with easy access to transportation. Many luxury hotels are also renowned for their unique and iconic architecture and design.

Some hotels are housed in historic buildings, while others feature ultra-modern design and cutting-edge technology.

Accommodations

Luxury hotels offer a range of accommodation options, from standard rooms to suites and villas. Rooms are often spacious and feature high-end amenities such as premium bedding, luxury toiletries, and state-of-the-art entertainment systems. Many luxury hotels also offer private balconies or terraces with stunning views.

Suites and villas are often the epitome of luxury accommodations, featuring multiple rooms, private outdoor spaces, and exclusive access to hotel amenities. Some luxury hotels also offer specialty suites that cater to specific needs, such as spa suites with private treatment rooms or penthouse suites with rooftop pools.

Service

One of the defining features of luxury hotels is their level of service. These hotels typically have highly trained staff who are dedicated to providing personalized service to guests. Many luxury hotels have a high staff-to-guest ratio, ensuring that every need is taken care of promptly and efficiently. Staff may offer personalized greetings and remember guest preferences, such as favorite foods or drinks.

Dining and Bars

Luxury hotels often feature world-class restaurants and bars, with award-winning chefs and innovative cuisine. Many hotels have multiple dining options, including fine dining restaurants, casual cafes, and room service. Bars and lounges are often designed to create a sophisticated atmosphere, with craft cocktails and premium spirits.

Spa and Wellness

Luxury hotels often feature high-end spa and wellness facilities, with a focus on relaxation and rejuvenation. Spas may offer a range of treatments, such as massages, facials, and body scrubs, as well as hydrotherapy pools and saunas. Many luxury hotels also have fitness centers with state-of-the-art equipment and personal trainers.

Activities and Entertainment

Luxury hotels often offer a range of activities and entertainment options, catering to guests of all ages and interests. These may include outdoor activities such as hiking or golfing, cultural tours or performances, or on-site activities such as cooking classes or wine tastings. Many luxury hotels also have exclusive partnerships with local attractions or cultural institutions, offering guests unique and exclusive experiences.

Technology

Luxury hotels often incorporate cutting-edge technology into their accommodations and amenities. This may include in-room entertainment systems with high-definition TVs and surround sound, smart home technology for controlling lighting and temperature, and high-speed internet access. Some hotels also offer virtual concierge services or mobile check-in, making the guest experience more seamless and convenient.

In conclusion, luxury hotels offer a unique and unforgettable experience for travelers who are seeking the best of the best when it comes to accommodations, service, and amenities. From prime locations and stunning design to personalized service and world-class dining, these hotels are the epitome of luxury hospitality. Whether you are traveling for business or pleasure, a stay at a luxury hotel is sure to be an unforgettable experience.

• Chapter 7: Budget and Economy Hotels

Budget and economy hotels are a popular option for travelers who are looking for affordable lodging options. These hotels offer basic accommodations and amenities at a lower price point than luxury hotels, making them a practical choice for budget-conscious travelers. In this article, we will explore the various aspects that make budget and economy hotels unique and desirable.

Location and Design

Budget and economy hotels are typically located in urban or suburban areas, near transportation hubs such as airports or train stations. These hotels are often designed to be functional and practical, with minimalist decor and basic furnishings. Some budget hotels may also offer shared accommodations, such as dormitory-style rooms with bunk beds, which can be an affordable option for solo travelers or groups.

Accommodations

Budget and economy hotels offer a range of accommodations, from standard rooms to suites and apartments. Rooms are typically smaller than those found in luxury hotels, with basic amenities such as a bed, a small desk, and a bathroom with a shower. Some budget hotels may also offer rooms with shared bathrooms, which can be an affordable option for travelers who are comfortable with communal facilities.

Suites and apartments are often larger and more spacious, with additional amenities such as a kitchenette or a living room area. These accommodations may be suitable for families or groups who are looking for a more comfortable and convenient lodging option.

Service

Budget and economy hotels offer a lower level of service than luxury hotels, but still provide basic amenities such as housekeeping, front desk assistance, and free Wi-Fi. Staff are typically friendly and helpful, but may not offer personalized service or special requests such as room service or concierge assistance.

Dining and Bars

Budget and economy hotels may offer a basic breakfast buffet or a small cafe or restaurant on site, but typically do not offer high-end dining options. Some hotels may also have a bar or lounge area where guests can relax and socialize.

Spa and Wellness

Budget and economy hotels typically do not offer spa or wellness facilities, but may have basic fitness centers or swimming pools. These amenities may be suitable for travelers who are looking for a simple and affordable way to stay active during their trip.

Activities and Entertainment

Budget and economy hotels may offer basic activities and entertainment options, such as board games or a small library. These hotels may also have partnerships with local attractions or tour companies, offering guests discounted tickets or packages for nearby activities.

Technology

Budget and economy hotels typically offer basic technology amenities, such as free Wi-Fi and flat-screen TVs. Some hotels may also offer charging ports or business centers for guests who need to work remotely or stay connected during their trip.

In conclusion, budget and economy hotels offer a practical and affordable lodging option for travelers who are looking for basic accommodations and amenities. These hotels may not offer the same level of luxury or personalized service as high-end hotels, but can still provide a comfortable and convenient stay.

Whether you are traveling for business or pleasure, a budget or economy hotel can be a practical and affordable way to enjoy your trip without breaking the bank.

• Chapter 8: Resort Hotels and Spas

Resort hotels and spas are popular lodging options for travelers who are looking for a relaxing and rejuvenating vacation experience. These hotels offer a range of amenities and services that can include luxurious accommodations, on-site restaurants and bars, swimming pools, spa facilities, fitness centers, and outdoor recreational activities. In this article, we will explore the various aspects that make resort hotels and spas unique and desirable.

Location and Design

Resort hotels and spas are typically located in scenic areas such as beaches, mountains, or forests. The design of these hotels is often influenced by the surrounding landscape, with natural materials and earthy tones used in the decor. Many resort hotels also have large outdoor spaces, such as gardens, courtyards, or terraces, that provide guests with a relaxing and peaceful atmosphere.

Accommodations

Resort hotels and spas offer a range of accommodations, from standard rooms to luxury suites and villas. Rooms are often spacious and well-appointed, with amenities such as comfortable bedding, high-quality linens, and luxury toiletries. Some resort hotels may also offer unique accommodations, such as treehouses, yurts, or beachfront bungalows.

Suites and villas are often larger and more luxurious than standard rooms, with additional amenities such as private pools, outdoor showers, or hot tubs. These accommodations may be suitable for couples or families who are looking for a more intimate and exclusive lodging experience.

Service

Resort hotels and spas offer a high level of service, with staff who are trained to provide personalized attention and assistance to guests. Services may include concierge assistance, room service, and daily housekeeping. Some resort hotels may also offer butler or valet services, which can add an extra level of luxury and convenience to a guest's stay.

Dining and Bars

Resort hotels and spas typically have multiple on-site dining options, ranging from casual cafes to high-end restaurants. These restaurants often feature locally-sourced ingredients and international cuisine, with menus that are designed to cater to a range of tastes and dietary preferences. Many resort hotels also have bars and lounges, where guests can enjoy a range of cocktails, wines, and spirits in a relaxed and comfortable atmosphere.

Spa and Wellness

Spa and wellness facilities are a key feature of resort hotels and spas, with many hotels offering a range of treatments and services such as massages, facials, body treatments, and hydrotherapy. Some resort hotels may also have outdoor hot springs, steam rooms, or saunas, which can provide guests with a unique and relaxing experience. Fitness centers and yoga studios may also be available, allowing guests to stay active and maintain their wellness routine while on vacation.

Activities and Entertainment

Resort hotels and spas offer a range of recreational activities and entertainment options, such as swimming pools, tennis courts, golf courses, and hiking trails. Some hotels may also offer water sports such as kayaking, paddleboarding, or sailing. Cultural activities such as cooking classes or art workshops may also be available, allowing guests to learn about the local culture and traditions.

Technology

Resort hotels and spas typically offer advanced technology amenities, such as high-speed Wi-Fi, flat-screen TVs, and Bluetooth speakers. Some hotels may also offer smart home technology, allowing guests to control various aspects of their room, such as the lighting, temperature, and entertainment options, through a mobile app or tablet.

In conclusion, resort hotels and spas offer a luxurious and rejuvenating vacation experience for travelers who are looking to escape the stress and chaos of daily life. These hotels provide a range of amenities and services that can cater to a variety of interests and preferences, allowing guests to relax and unwind in a beautiful and serene setting.

• Chapter 9: Business Hotels and Conference Centers

Business hotels and conference centers cater primarily to business travelers who need access to modern amenities, business services, and meeting facilities.

They are designed to provide comfort and convenience to busy professionals, with the aim of making their stay as productive as possible.

Location:

Business hotels are usually located in or near business districts, close to transportation hubs, such as airports and train stations, and are often close to major conference centers or other business venues.

Facilities:

Business hotels are well-equipped with facilities that cater to the needs of business travelers. These facilities often include fully equipped business centers with computer terminals, printers, fax machines, and other office equipment. High-speed internet and Wi-Fi access are essential for business travelers, so these services are usually available throughout the hotel. Many hotels offer meeting rooms and conference facilities, which can accommodate groups of various sizes. The rooms are usually equipped with audio-visual equipment, such as projectors and screens, to facilitate presentations and discussions.

Accommodations:

Rooms in business hotels are designed to be comfortable and functional. They are equipped with modern amenities such as large flat-screen televisions, work desks, and ergonomic chairs. Some hotels also offer executive floors, which provide additional services such as a private lounge, complimentary breakfast, and evening cocktails. Rooms may also feature a coffee maker, mini-fridge, and microwave for added convenience.

Food and Beverage:

Business hotels usually have at least one restaurant, offering a range of cuisine to suit different tastes. Many hotels also have a bar or lounge, providing a relaxed atmosphere where guests can socialize or conduct informal meetings. Room service is usually available around the clock for guests who prefer to dine in the privacy of their own rooms.

Other services:

Business hotels often offer additional services, such as a fitness center, swimming pool, or spa facilities. These services allow guests to unwind after a long day of meetings and work. Some hotels also offer a concierge service, which can assist guests with travel arrangements, restaurant reservations, and other needs.

Marketing:

Business hotels target business travelers through marketing campaigns that emphasize their facilities and services, as well as their location and accessibility. They also market themselves to meeting and event planners, highlighting their conference facilities and catering services.

In conclusion, business hotels and conference centers are an essential part of the hospitality industry, catering to the needs of business travelers who require comfortable accommodations, modern amenities, and convenient access to business facilities. With their well-equipped meeting rooms and conference facilities, these hotels play a crucial role in hosting meetings, events, and conventions, making them an integral part of the business world.

. Chapter 10: Extended Stay Hotels and Serviced Apartments

Extended stay hotels and serviced apartments are designed to provide comfortable, long-term accommodations for travelers who need to stay in one place for an extended period of time. These types of lodging options offer more space and amenities than traditional hotels, making them ideal for business travelers, families, and individuals who need a home-away-from-home experience.

Location:

Extended stay hotels and serviced apartments are typically located in or near business districts, residential neighborhoods, and tourist areas. They are often situated near public transportation or major highways, making it easy for guests to get around the city.

Facilities:

Extended stay hotels and serviced apartments offer a range of facilities that cater to the needs of long-term guests. These facilities may include a fully equipped kitchen, a separate living room or sitting area, and a dining table. Many extended stay hotels also offer on-site laundry facilities, a fitness center, and a business center with printing and fax services.

Accommodations:

Extended stay hotels and serviced apartments offer a range of accommodations to suit different needs and budgets. Studio apartments are the most basic option, offering a combined living and sleeping area with a kitchenette and bathroom. One-bedroom apartments provide separate living and sleeping areas, while two-bedroom apartments are ideal for families or groups traveling together.

Food and Beverage:

Extended stay hotels and serviced apartments usually offer a complimentary breakfast, and some properties may offer an on-site restaurant or café. However, the primary advantage of these accommodations is the ability to prepare meals in the fully equipped kitchen, which can save guests money on dining expenses.

Other services:

Extended stay hotels and serviced apartments offer additional services that are not typically found in traditional hotels. Some properties offer a grocery delivery service, allowing guests to order groceries online and have them delivered to their room. Many properties also offer housekeeping services, though these services are typically offered on a weekly or bi-weekly basis, rather than daily.

Marketing:

Extended stay hotels and serviced apartments target guests who need long-term accommodations, such as business travelers, relocating families, and those on extended vacations. These properties are marketed through a variety of channels, including online travel agencies, social media, and direct marketing to corporate clients.

In conclusion, extended stay hotels and serviced apartments offer a comfortable and convenient alternative to traditional hotels, catering to the needs of long-term guests who require more space and amenities. These properties provide a home-away-from-home experience, allowing guests to prepare their own meals, do their own laundry, and enjoy the privacy and flexibility of their own space. With their range of accommodations and facilities, extended stay hotels and serviced apartments are an important part of the hospitality industry, serving a diverse range of travelers and meeting a variety of needs.

Section 3: Operations and Management of Hotels

Operations and management are critical components of any hotel's success. To ensure that a hotel runs smoothly and efficiently, there are a number of key areas that must be managed effectively, from front desk operations to housekeeping, maintenance, and food and beverage service.

Front Desk Operations:

The front desk is the first point of contact for guests, and it is critical to ensure that it is staffed by friendly and knowledgeable employees who can handle guest inquiries, check-ins, and check-outs efficiently. The front desk is also responsible for managing reservations, managing room assignments, and handling billing and payments.

Housekeeping:

The housekeeping department is responsible for ensuring that guest rooms are clean, comfortable, and well-maintained. Housekeepers must be skilled in a range of tasks, from changing linens to cleaning bathrooms and replenishing amenities. Effective communication between the front desk and housekeeping staff is critical to ensure that rooms are ready for new guests as soon as possible.

Maintenance:

The maintenance department is responsible for ensuring that the hotel's physical plant is in good working order, from plumbing and electrical systems to HVAC and structural maintenance. Maintenance staff must be skilled in a range of trades and able to respond to issues promptly and efficiently to minimize disruption to guests.

Food and Beverage Service:

Many hotels offer on-site dining options, including restaurants, cafes, and bars. These facilities are typically managed by a food and beverage manager, who is responsible for overseeing menu development, food and beverage service, inventory management, and staffing. Effective management of food and beverage operations is critical to ensuring a positive guest experience and generating revenue for the hotel.

Marketing and Sales:

Effective marketing and sales strategies are critical to the success of any hotel. Marketing efforts may include online advertising, social media campaigns, and partnerships with travel agencies and tour operators. Sales staff are responsible for developing relationships with corporate clients, meeting planners, and travel agents to generate business for the hotel.

Human Resources:

Effective management of human resources is critical to ensuring that a hotel runs smoothly and that employees are motivated and engaged. The human resources department is responsible for recruitment and selection, training and development, performance management, and employee relations. Effective management of human resources can help to minimize turnover, improve employee morale, and ensure that the hotel's workforce is aligned with its strategic goals.

Financial Management:

Effective financial management is critical to the success of any hotel. Financial managers must be skilled in budgeting, forecasting, and financial analysis to ensure that the hotel is profitable and financially stable. They must also ensure that the hotel complies with regulatory requirements and tax laws.In conclusion, effective operations and management are critical to the success of any hotel. By ensuring that front desk operations, housekeeping, maintenance, food and beverage service, marketing and sales, human resources, and financial management are all managed effectively, hotels can provide a positive guest experience, generate revenue, and maintain financial stability. Skilled managers and staff, effective communication, and a commitment to excellence are all essential components of effective hotel operations and management.

Chapter 11: Revenue Management and Pricing Strategies

Revenue management and pricing strategies are critical components of a hotel's success. The goal of revenue management is to maximize revenue by balancing supply and demand and adjusting prices accordingly. In order to do this effectively, hotels must understand their target market, competition, and demand patterns.

Forecasting Demand:

Forecasting demand is a critical component of revenue management. Hotels must be able to predict future demand in order to make informed decisions about pricing and inventory. Demand forecasting involves analyzing historical data, trends, and external factors such as seasonality, events, and market trends.

Inventory Management:

Effective inventory management is critical to revenue management. Hotels must balance the number of rooms available with the level of demand in order to maximize revenue. This involves carefully managing room allocations and adjusting pricing based on demand. Dynamic pricing algorithms can help hotels to adjust pricing in real time based on demand.

Pricing Strategies:

There are a number of pricing strategies that hotels can use to maximize revenue. These include dynamic pricing, which involves adjusting prices in real time based on demand, and yield management, which involves adjusting prices based on supply and demand. Other pricing strategies include seasonal pricing, which involves adjusting prices based on seasonality, and segmentation pricing, which involves adjusting prices based on different market segments.

Channel Management:

Channel management involves managing the distribution channels through which a hotel sells its rooms. Effective channel management can help hotels to reach their target market and maximize revenue. Channels may include online travel agencies, direct bookings, and corporate contracts. Effective channel management involves analyzing the performance of each channel and adjusting strategies accordingly.

Data Analysis:

Effective data analysis is critical to revenue management. Hotels must be able to collect and analyze data on room rates, occupancy rates, and demand patterns in order to make informed decisions about pricing and inventory management. Data analysis may involve the use of data mining, predictive analytics, and business intelligence tools.

Marketing and Sales:

Effective marketing and sales strategies can also play a role in revenue management. Hotels must be able to reach their target market and effectively communicate the value of their offerings. Effective marketing strategies may include online advertising, social media campaigns, and partnerships with travel agencies and tour operators. Sales staff may also play a role in revenue management by developing relationships with corporate clients, meeting planners, and travel agents to generate business for the hotel.

In conclusion, revenue management and pricing strategies are critical components of a hotel's success. Effective revenue management involves forecasting demand, managing inventory, implementing pricing strategies, managing channels, analyzing data, and developing effective marketing and sales strategies. By managing these components effectively, hotels can maximize revenue, maintain profitability, and provide a positive guest experience. Skilled revenue managers, effective communication, and a commitment to data analysis and continuous improvement are all essential components of effective revenue management and pricing strategies in the hotel industry.

• Chapter 12: Marketing and Branding for Hotels

Marketing and branding are essential for hotels to attract guests and establish a strong reputation. Effective marketing and branding strategies can help hotels to differentiate themselves from competitors, increase brand awareness, and generate business. In this article, we will discuss the key components of effective marketing and branding for hotels.

Market Research:

Market research is a critical component of effective marketing and branding. Hotels must be able to understand their target market and their needs in order to develop effective marketing strategies. Market research may involve analyzing industry trends, guest feedback, and competitor analysis. This information can be used to develop targeted marketing campaigns and identify opportunities for differentiation.

Brand Identity:

A strong brand identity is essential for hotels to establish a unique position in the market. A hotel's brand identity includes its name, logo, tagline, and overall visual identity. Hotels must ensure that their brand identity is consistent across all channels, including their website, social media profiles, and physical properties. A strong brand identity can help to build trust and recognition with guests.

Website and Online Presence:

A hotel's website and online presence are essential components of its marketing strategy. A hotel's website should be visually appealing, easy to navigate, and provide all the necessary information for guests to make a booking. It should also be optimized for search engines, so that it appears high in search results when potential guests are searching for hotels in the area. In addition to the website, hotels should have a strong presence on social media platforms, online travel agencies, and review sites.

Advertising and Promotions:

Advertising and promotions are essential components of a hotel's marketing strategy. Hotels may use a variety of channels to promote their offerings, including online advertising, print advertising, and email marketing. Promotions may include discounts, packages, and special offers. Hotels may also partner with travel agencies, airlines, and other businesses to offer joint promotions.

Public Relations:

Public relations can play an important role in building a hotel's reputation and generating media coverage. Hotels may issue press releases, host media events, and offer media familiarization trips to journalists and bloggers. Positive media coverage can help to build brand awareness and establish a positive reputation in the industry.

Guest Experience:

The guest experience is one of the most important components of effective marketing and branding. A positive guest experience can lead to positive reviews, word-of-mouth referrals, and repeat business. Hotels must ensure that they provide a high level of service, personalized attention, and a welcoming environment to all guests.

In conclusion, effective marketing and branding are essential components of a hotel's success. Key components of effective marketing and branding include market research, brand identity, website and online presence, advertising and promotions, public relations, and guest experience. By focusing on these components, hotels can establish a strong reputation, differentiate themselves from competitors, and attract and retain guests. A strong brand identity, effective communication, and a commitment to providing a positive guest experience are all essential components of effective marketing and branding in the hotel industry.

• Chapter 13: Customer Service and Guest Experience

Customer service and guest experience are two critical aspects of the hotel industry that can make or break a hotel's success. In the hospitality industry, guests' satisfaction and comfort are the primary concern of hotels, and this can be achieved through excellent customer service and guest experience.

Customer service in hotels involves all interactions between the guests and the hotel staff, including reception, room service, restaurant service, housekeeping, and other amenities. The primary objective of customer service in hotels is to ensure that guests are satisfied with their stay and that all their needs are met promptly and efficiently. This includes providing assistance with transportation, luggage, and other requirements that guests may have during their stay.

Guest experience, on the other hand, refers to the overall experience that guests have during their stay in a hotel. It encompasses everything from the moment they arrive until they leave, including the quality of service, the amenities provided, the cleanliness and comfort of the rooms, the ambiance, and the quality of food and beverage services. A positive guest experience can lead to repeat business and positive reviews, while a negative experience can lead to loss of business and a negative reputation for the hotel.

Effective customer service and guest experience require the hotel staff to be attentive, responsive, and knowledgeable. They should be well-trained to handle any issues that may arise during a guest's stay and should be able to provide quick and efficient solutions. This includes resolving complaints, providing recommendations for local attractions and restaurants, and accommodating any special requests or needs that guests may have.

To achieve high levels of customer service and guest experience, hotels often invest in staff training programs and regularly review and evaluate their service quality. They also use guest feedback and reviews to identify areas that need improvement and to make necessary changes.

In addition, hotels use various tools and strategies to enhance the guest experience, including the use of technology, such as mobile check-in and keyless entry systems, in-room tablets, and personalized digital concierge services. They also offer additional amenities such as fitness centers, spas, and entertainment options to provide guests with a unique and memorable experience.

Marketing and branding also play a crucial role in creating a positive guest experience. Hotels use various marketing strategies to attract and retain customers, including online and offline advertising, loyalty programs, and social media marketing. Branding, on the other hand, involves creating a unique identity and personality for the hotel and creating a strong brand image that guests can identify with and trust.

In conclusion, customer service and guest experience are two critical aspects of the hotel industry that are essential for a hotel's success. Hotels that provide excellent customer service and a positive guest experience can gain a competitive edge and achieve long-term success. By investing in staff training, using technology, and enhancing their amenities, hotels can create a memorable and unique guest experience that can lead to repeat business and positive reviews.

• Chapter 14: Human Resources and Employee Management

Human resources and employee management play a critical role in the success of any hotel operation. In the hotel industry, employees are the face of the business, and their performance can greatly impact the guest experience. Therefore, it is essential to have effective human resource policies and management strategies in place to recruit, train, and retain top-performing employees.

Recruitment and Selection:

Recruiting and selecting employees is the first step in building a successful team. Hotels must ensure that they attract a diverse pool of candidates by creating job postings that are clear, concise, and inclusive. Recruitment can be done through various channels, such as job portals, social media, and employee referrals.

Once a pool of candidates has been identified, hotels need to conduct a thorough selection process to identify the best candidates for the job. This can include conducting interviews, administering tests, and checking references. It is also important to ensure that the recruitment process is fair and unbiased, and that all candidates are treated equally.

Training and Development:

Once employees have been recruited, hotels must provide them with the necessary training and development opportunities to perform their job effectively. This includes both job-specific training and broader professional development opportunities. Job-specific training can include learning about hotel policies and procedures, operating hotel equipment, and customer service skills. Professional development opportunities can include attending conferences, workshops, and online courses.

Hotels should also provide ongoing training and development opportunities to ensure that employees are continuously improving their skills and knowledge. This can include cross-training employees in different departments, providing leadership training for supervisors, and offering tuition reimbursement for employees who want to pursue further education.

Compensation and Benefits:

Hotels must offer competitive compensation and benefits packages to attract and retain top-performing employees. Compensation can include base pay, bonuses, and commissions. Benefits can include health insurance, retirement plans, and paid time off. Hotels should regularly review their compensation and benefits packages to ensure that they remain competitive with other hotels in the industry.

Employee Engagement:

Employee engagement is essential for creating a positive work culture and retaining employees. Hotels can foster employee engagement by creating a positive work environment, providing opportunities for employee feedback and input, and recognizing and rewarding employee achievements. Employee engagement can also be increased by providing opportunities for career advancement, offering flexible work arrangements, and promoting work-life balance.

Employee Retention:

Employee retention is a critical aspect of effective employee management. Retaining employees can save hotels time and money associated with recruiting and training new employees. To retain employees, hotels must ensure that they provide opportunities for career advancement, a positive work culture, and competitive compensation and benefits. Hotels should also provide ongoing feedback and recognition to employees and listen to their concerns and suggestions.

Employee Performance Management:

Managing employee performance is a critical aspect of effective employee management. Hotels should have a performance management system in place that includes regular performance reviews, setting performance goals, and providing ongoing feedback and coaching. Employee performance should be measured against clear, objective criteria, and employees should be given opportunities to improve their performance when necessary.

In conclusion, effective human resources and employee management are essential for the success of hotels. By recruiting top-performing employees, providing effective training and development opportunities, offering competitive compensation and benefits, fostering employee engagement, retaining employees, and managing employee performance, hotels can create a positive work culture and provide a superior guest experience.

• Chapter 15: Hotel Operations and Maintenance

Hotel Operations and Maintenance refer to the day-to-day activities and tasks that keep a hotel running smoothly and ensure that guests have a comfortable and enjoyable stay. These operations and maintenance activities include a range of tasks, from housekeeping and maintenance to front desk operations and guest services. In this article, we will explore the various aspects of hotel operations and maintenance and how they contribute to the success of a hotel.

Front Desk Operations

The front desk is the nerve center of any hotel. It is where guests check-in and check-out, make reservations, and seek assistance for any needs during their stay. Front desk personnel are responsible for providing guests with a warm and welcoming experience and ensuring that their needs are met promptly and efficiently. This includes answering questions, providing directions and recommendations, and resolving any issues or complaints that may arise. Front desk staff must have excellent communication skills, be knowledgeable about the hotel's amenities and services, and be able to handle multiple tasks simultaneously.

Housekeeping

Housekeeping is a critical function in hotel operations and maintenance. It involves the cleaning and maintenance of guest rooms, public spaces, and back-of-the-house areas. Housekeeping staff are responsible for ensuring that guest rooms are cleaned and maintained to a high standard, that supplies and amenities are stocked, and that guest requests are fulfilled promptly. They also play a critical role in maintaining the overall cleanliness and hygiene of the hotel.

Maintenance

Maintenance is another crucial aspect of hotel operations and maintenance. It involves the repair and upkeep of the hotel's physical assets, including the building, equipment, and grounds. Maintenance staff are responsible for ensuring that the hotel's facilities are safe, functional, and aesthetically pleasing. This includes performing routine maintenance tasks, such as changing light bulbs and air filters, as well as more complex repairs, such as fixing plumbing or electrical systems.

Food and Beverage Operations

Food and beverage operations are a critical component of many hotels, particularly those that offer dining services. These operations include the management of restaurants, bars, banquet facilities, and room service. Food and beverage staff are responsible for ensuring that guests have an enjoyable dining experience, from the quality of the food and drink to the ambiance and service.

Guest Services

Guest services are a broad category that encompasses a range of functions, from concierge services to valet parking. Guest service staff are responsible for providing guests with assistance and support during their stay, from arranging transportation to making recommendations for local activities and attractions. They must be knowledgeable about the hotel and the local area and able to handle guest requests and concerns promptly and efficiently.

Security

Security is an essential component of hotel operations and maintenance. Hotel security personnel are responsible for ensuring the safety and security of guests, employees, and the hotel's assets. This includes monitoring access to the hotel and its facilities, responding to emergencies and incidents, and enforcing hotel policies and procedures.Overall, hotel operations and maintenance are critical to the success of any hotel. They involve a range of tasks and responsibilities that require skilled and knowledgeable staff to carry out effectively.

Section 4: Current Trends and Challenges in the Hotel Industry

The hotel industry is constantly evolving to keep up with changing consumer preferences and new technological advancements. In this section, we will discuss the current trends and challenges facing the hotel industry.

Technology Integration:

1. One of the most significant trends in the hotel industry is the integration of technology into hotel operations. Guests expect seamless access

to technology, including high-speed internet, mobile check-in and check-out, and digital key access. Hotels are investing in technology to provide guests with more personalized experiences, such as mobile apps that offer recommendations on local attractions and dining options, and the use of artificial intelligence to predict guest preferences.

Sustainability:

2. Sustainability has become a significant trend in the hotel industry. Consumers are becoming more environmentally conscious and are looking for eco-friendly options when choosing a hotel. Many hotels are adopting sustainable practices, such as reducing water and energy consumption, using locally sourced materials, and offering guests the option to reuse towels and linens. Sustainability is not only good for the environment, but it is also cost-effective for hotels in the long run.

Rise of Boutique and Lifestyle Hotels:

3. Boutique and lifestyle hotels are gaining popularity among travelers. These hotels offer unique experiences that cater to specific target

markets, such as millennials or luxury travelers. Boutique hotels typically have fewer rooms and offer a more intimate atmosphere, while lifestyle hotels offer guests a range of experiences, including wellness, fitness, and cultural activities.

Increased Emphasis on Health and Wellness:

4. The health and wellness trend is rapidly growing in the hotel industry. Many hotels are offering guests wellness experiences such as yoga classes, spa treatments, and healthy dining options. Wellness-focused hotels are also incorporating technology, such as sleep-monitoring devices and fitness trackers, to help guests track their health and fitness goals.

Short-Term Rentals:

5. Short-term rentals, such as those offered through platforms like Airbnb, are increasingly popular among travelers. Many hotels are struggling to compete with the lower prices and more authentic experiences offered by short-term rentals. As a result, hotels are exploring ways to integrate short-term rentals into their operations, such as partnering with Airbnb to offer hotel-

quality services to guests staying in Airbnb accommodations.

Labor Shortages:

6. Labor shortages are one of the most significant challenges facing the hotel industry. The industry relies heavily on a workforce that is often low-paid and undervalued. As a result, hotels are finding it increasingly difficult to attract and retain skilled workers. Some hotels are investing in training and development programs to help retain staff, while others are exploring the use of automation and robotics to fill labor gaps.

Changing Consumer Preferences:

7. The preferences of consumers are constantly changing, and hotels must keep up with these changes to remain competitive. For example, millennials tend to value experiences over material possessions, and hotels must offer unique experiences that cater to this demographic. Similarly, consumers are becoming more interested in authentic, local experiences, and hotels must offer local

recommendations and experiences to meet these preferences.

Safety and Security:

8. Safety and security have become increasingly important to travelers, particularly in the wake of global events such as terrorist attacks and natural disasters. Hotels must ensure that they have robust safety and security measures in place to protect their guests and staff. This includes measures such as increased security personnel, CCTV surveillance, and emergency response plans.

In conclusion, the hotel industry is constantly evolving to meet the changing needs and preferences of consumers. The integration of technology, sustainability, and unique experiences are some of the significant trends shaping the industry. However, challenges such as labor shortages, changing consumer preferences, and safety and security concerns remain significant challenges for the industry. It is essential for hotels to stay current with these trends and challenges to remain competitive and meet the needs of their guests.

Chapter 16: Sustainability in Hotels

Sustainability in hotels is a topic of increasing importance in the modern world. As more and more people become concerned about the impact that human activity is having on the environment, the hotel industry has begun to respond with initiatives aimed at reducing their carbon footprint, protecting local ecosystems, and promoting sustainable practices.

Sustainable practices in hotels can take many different forms, from energy-efficient lighting and heating systems to recycling programs and water conservation measures. One of the key challenges faced by hotels when it comes to sustainability is finding a balance between minimizing their environmental impact while still providing a high level of service to guests.

One area where hotels can make a significant impact on sustainability is in their use of resources such as water and energy. Water conservation measures can include everything from low-flow toilets and showerheads to rainwater harvesting systems, which can help to reduce water usage and preserve local water resources.

Similarly, hotels can reduce their energy usage through a range of measures, such as installing energy-efficient lighting and HVAC systems, using renewable energy sources like solar or wind power, and implementing smart controls to reduce energy consumption when rooms are unoccupied.

Another key area where hotels can make a difference is in the sourcing of their food and other supplies. Many hotels are now making a concerted effort to source their products locally, reducing the carbon footprint associated with transporting goods from distant locations. They are also choosing suppliers that use sustainable farming and fishing practices, avoiding products that are produced in ways that damage the environment.

Hotels can also promote sustainability through guest engagement and education. Many hotels are now providing guests with information about their sustainable practices and encouraging them to participate in activities like recycling and water conservation. Some hotels even offer sustainability-themed packages, giving guests the opportunity to learn more about sustainable practices while enjoying their stay.

Sustainability in hotels is not without its challenges, however. One of the key obstacles faced by hotels is the upfront cost of implementing sustainable practices. While many sustainability initiatives will ultimately save money over the long term, there is often a significant upfront investment required to install energy-efficient systems or to implement recycling programs, for example.

Another challenge is the need to balance sustainability goals with the desire to provide a high level of service to guests. While sustainable practices like low-flow showerheads and energy-efficient lighting can help to reduce a hotel's environmental impact, they may also result in a less luxurious experience for guests, which could impact their satisfaction and willingness to return.

Finally, there is the challenge of measuring the impact of sustainability initiatives. While it is relatively easy to track things like energy and water usage, it can be more difficult to quantify the broader impact of sustainable practices on the environment and local communities.

Despite these challenges, however, sustainability is becoming an increasingly important focus for hotels around the world. As guests become more concerned about the environment and the impact of their travel, hotels are recognizing the importance of taking action to reduce their carbon footprint and promote sustainable practices. By embracing sustainability, hotels can not only reduce their impact on the environment but also improve their reputation and appeal to guests who are looking for environmentally responsible travel options.

· Chapter 17: Technology and Innovation

Technology and innovation have significantly impacted the hotel industry in recent years. From online bookings to mobile check-ins, hotels are leveraging technology to provide better services, enhance the guest experience, and improve operational efficiency. This article will discuss the various ways technology and innovation are transforming the hotel industry.

1. Online Bookings and Reservations

The rise of online travel agencies (OTAs) such as Booking.com, Expedia, and Airbnb has disrupted the traditional booking process in the hotel industry. Guests can now book their rooms online through various platforms, making it easier and more convenient for them to make reservations. Hotels are also investing in their websites to provide a user-friendly and seamless booking experience for guests.

2. Mobile Technology

The use of mobile technology has revolutionized the way hotels operate. Guests can now use their mobile devices to check-in, unlock their room doors, and access hotel amenities. Mobile apps also allow guests to make requests and communicate with hotel staff. Hotels are also using mobile technology to personalize the guest experience by offering customized recommendations and personalized offers.

3. Smart Rooms

Smart rooms are becoming more common in hotels, allowing guests to control various aspects of their room, such as lighting, temperature, and entertainment systems, using their mobile devices. Hotels are also using smart technology to monitor energy usage and reduce waste, thus promoting sustainability.

4. Artificial Intelligence (AI) and Chatbots

AI is becoming increasingly prevalent in the hotel industry, with chatbots being used to provide instant responses to guests' queries and requests. Chatbots can also be used to provide recommendations and personalized offers to guests based on their preferences and previous interactions with the hotel.

5. Virtual and Augmented Reality

Virtual and augmented reality are being used in the hotel industry to provide guests with a preview of their rooms and hotel amenities. This technology allows guests to explore the hotel virtually before they arrive, enhancing the guest experience and increasing the likelihood of booking a room.

6. Data Analytics

Data analytics is being used by hotels to gain insights into guest behavior and preferences. This information can be used to personalize the guest experience and tailor offers and recommendations to individual guests. Data analytics can also be used to improve operational efficiency and reduce costs.

7. Contactless Payments

The COVID-19 pandemic has accelerated the adoption of contactless payments in the hotel industry. Guests can now use their mobile devices to make payments, reducing the need for physical contact and promoting social distancing.

Challenges

While technology and innovation have transformed the hotel industry, they have also presented several challenges. One of the biggest challenges is the cost of implementing new technology and training staff to use it effectively. Hotels must also ensure that they maintain a balance between technology and human interaction, as some guests still prefer to interact with hotel staff directly.

Another challenge is data security and privacy. Hotels must ensure that they protect guest data and comply with data protection regulations.

Conclusion

Technology and innovation have transformed the hotel industry, enabling hotels to provide better services, enhance the guest experience, and improve operational efficiency. Hotels must continue to embrace new technology and trends to remain competitive in the industry. However, it is essential that hotels strike a balance between technology and human interaction to provide a personalized and memorable experience for their guests.

• Chapter 18: The Impact of the COVID-19 Pandemic

The COVID-19 pandemic has had a significant impact on the world in many ways. It has affected nearly every aspect of life, from health and the economy to social interactions and daily routines. In this essay, we will explore the impact of the COVID-19 pandemic on various aspects of society and discuss the measures taken to mitigate its effects.

Health Impact

The COVID-19 pandemic has had a devastating impact on public health. The virus is highly contagious and has spread rapidly throughout the world, leading to millions of infections and deaths. The pandemic has overwhelmed healthcare systems, particularly in countries with limited resources.

The pandemic has also highlighted the importance of public health measures, such as wearing masks, social distancing, and frequent hand washing. Governments and health organizations around the world have implemented measures to control the spread of the virus, such as lockdowns and travel restrictions. These measures have been effective in slowing the spread of the virus, but they have also had significant economic and social consequences.

Economic Impact

The COVID-19 pandemic has had a significant impact on the global economy. Lockdowns and travel restrictions have led to the closure of businesses and the loss of jobs. The pandemic has affected many industries, including travel and tourism, hospitality, and retail. Many businesses have been forced to adapt to the changing circumstances, such as by offering online services or implementing new safety measures.

Governments around the world have implemented measures to support businesses and individuals affected by the pandemic. These measures have included stimulus packages, unemployment benefits, and loan programs. However, the economic impact of the pandemic is likely to be felt for many years to come.

Social Impact

The COVID-19 pandemic has had a significant impact on social interactions and daily routines. Lockdowns and travel restrictions have led to the closure of schools and workplaces, and many people have been forced to work from home or attend school online. The pandemic has also had an impact on mental health, with many people experiencing increased stress, anxiety, and depression.

The pandemic has also highlighted existing social inequalities. People from low-income backgrounds, minority groups, and those with underlying health conditions have been disproportionately affected by the pandemic. The pandemic has also led to an increase in domestic violence and child abuse, as families spend more time together in confined spaces.

· Chapter 19: Globalization and the Future of Hospitality

Globalization has had a significant impact on the hospitality industry. It has created new opportunities for growth, expanded markets, and increased competition. The future of the hospitality industry will continue to be shaped by globalization, as the world becomes more connected and accessible. In this essay, we will explore the impact of globalization on the hospitality industry and discuss the future trends and challenges.

Globalization in the Hospitality Industry

The hospitality industry includes a wide range of businesses, including hotels, restaurants, resorts, and tourism companies. Globalization has had a significant impact on each of these businesses, as it has opened up new markets and created new opportunities for growth.

One of the most significant impacts of globalization has been the increase in international tourism. As people become more connected and travel becomes more accessible, more people are traveling to different parts of the world. This has created new opportunities for hotels, resorts, and other hospitality businesses to cater to the needs of international travelers.

Another impact of globalization has been the increase in competition. As the world becomes more connected, businesses are no longer competing just with local businesses but with businesses from around the world. This has led to increased competition and has forced hospitality businesses to improve their services and offer unique experiences to attract customers.

Globalization has also had an impact on the workforce in the hospitality industry. As businesses expand and new markets are opened up, there is a greater need for a diverse workforce that can cater to the needs of international travelers. This has led to an increase in the hiring of employees from different cultural backgrounds and a greater emphasis on diversity and inclusion in the workplace.

Future Trends in the Hospitality Industry

The hospitality industry is constantly evolving, and there are several trends that are likely to shape its future. These trends include:

1. Technology: Technology has already had a significant impact on the hospitality industry, and this is likely to continue in the future. Hotels and resorts are likely to invest in new technologies, such as smart rooms and mobile check-in, to improve the guest experience.

2. Sustainability: There is an increasing emphasis on sustainability in the hospitality industry, as businesses look for ways to reduce their environmental impact. This includes initiatives such as reducing energy consumption, using renewable energy sources, and reducing waste.

3. Personalization: Customers are increasingly looking for personalized experiences, and the hospitality industry is likely to respond to this trend by offering more tailored experiences and services.

4. Wellness: There is a growing demand for wellness experiences in the hospitality industry, as customers look for ways to relax and recharge. This includes services such as spa

treatments, yoga classes, and healthy dining options.

5. Cultural experiences: As the world becomes more connected, there is a greater interest in cultural experiences. Hotels and resorts are likely to offer more cultural experiences, such as local tours and culinary experiences.

Challenges Facing the Hospitality Industry

Despite the many opportunities created by globalization, the hospitality industry also faces several challenges. These challenges include:

- Labor shortages: The hospitality industry is facing a shortage of skilled workers, particularly in areas such as culinary arts and housekeeping. This is likely to become an even greater challenge in the future as the industry continues to grow.

- Economic uncertainty: The hospitality industry is particularly vulnerable to economic downturns, as customers tend to cut back on travel during difficult economic times. The industry is likely to face continued economic uncertainty in the future, particularly in light of events such as the COVID-19 pandemic.

- Environmental concerns: The hospitality industry has a significant environmental impact, and businesses are under increasing pressure to reduce their impact on the environment. This is likely to become an even greater challenge in the future as businesses face stricter environmental regulations.

Chapter 20: Interviews with Industry Experts

Interviews with industry experts are an essential tool for gaining insight into various industries and staying up to date with current trends and developments. In this essay, we will discuss the importance of interviews with industry experts and provide some examples of how these interviews can provide valuable information.

Importance of Interviews with Industry Experts

Interviews with industry experts are valuable because they provide firsthand knowledge of an industry. These experts have years of experience and a wealth of knowledge about their industry, which they can share with others. Interviews can also provide insight into the latest trends and developments within an industry, which is particularly useful for businesses looking to stay ahead of the competition.

Interviews with industry experts can also be an effective way of generating publicity for a business or individual. By conducting interviews with industry experts, businesses and individuals can establish themselves as thought leaders within their industry, which can lead to increased visibility and credibility.

Examples of Interviews with Industry Experts

1. Technology Industry: An interview with an expert in the technology industry can provide insight into the latest technological advancements and trends. For example, an interview with a software developer could provide insight into the latest programming languages and development techniques, while an interview with a hardware engineer could provide insight into the latest advancements in computer hardware.

2. Hospitality Industry: An interview with an expert in the hospitality industry can provide insight into the latest trends in hospitality and travel. For example, an interview with a hotel manager could provide insight into the latest hotel

amenities and services, while an interview with a travel agent could provide insight into the latest travel trends and destinations.

3. Healthcare Industry: An interview with an expert in the healthcare industry can provide insight into the latest medical advancements and trends. For example, an interview with a medical researcher could provide insight into the latest treatments for various diseases, while an interview with a healthcare administrator could provide insight into the latest trends in healthcare management.

4. Marketing Industry: An interview with an expert in the marketing industry can provide insight into the latest marketing strategies and trends. For example, an interview with a social media expert could provide insight into the latest social media marketing strategies, while an interview with a branding expert could provide insight into the latest branding techniques.

5. Financial Industry: An interview with an expert in the financial industry can provide insight into the latest financial trends and developments. For example, an interview with a financial analyst

could provide insight into the latest stock market trends, while an interview with an investment banker could provide insight into the latest investment strategies.

Conclusion

Interviews with industry experts are a valuable tool for gaining insight into various industries and staying up to date with current trends and developments. These interviews can provide firsthand knowledge and insight into the latest advancements and trends, which can be useful for businesses and individuals looking to stay ahead of the competition. By conducting interviews with industry experts, businesses and individuals can establish themselves as thought leaders within their industry, which can lead to increased visibility and credibility.

Appendix:

- Glossary of Hotel Industry Terms

The hotel industry is a complex and dynamic industry with many specialized terms and jargon. In this glossary, we will define some of the most commonly used terms in the hotel industry.

1. ADR: Average Daily Rate - The average rate per room per day, calculated by dividing the total room revenue by the total number of rooms sold.

2. Occupancy Rate: The percentage of available rooms that are occupied during a specific period, usually measured on a daily, weekly or monthly basis.

3. RevPAR: Revenue per Available Room - Calculated by multiplying the ADR by the occupancy rate, this metric measures the average revenue generated per available room.

4. Yield Management: The practice of optimizing revenue by adjusting room rates based on demand, occupancy and other factors.

5. Housekeeping: The department responsible for cleaning and maintaining guest rooms, public areas, and other areas of the hotel.

6. Front Desk: The area of the hotel where guests check-in and check-out, make reservations, and receive information and assistance.

7. Concierge: A hotel employee who assists guests with arranging activities, transportation, dining reservations, and other services.

8. Room Service: The service of providing food and beverages to guests in their rooms, often 24 hours a day.

9. Banquet: A large gathering or event, usually involving food and beverage service, held in a hotel's banquet hall or meeting room.

10. Resort Fee: A mandatory fee charged by some hotels that covers amenities such as Wi-Fi, pool access, and fitness center use.

11. Hospitality Industry: The industry that encompasses all aspects of travel, tourism, and accommodations, including hotels, restaurants, transportation, and related businesses.

12. Guest Room: A room in a hotel that is rented out to guests for overnight stays.

13. Room Block: A group of rooms that are reserved for a specific event or group, often at a discounted rate.

14. Check-in: The process of registering at the hotel and receiving a room key.

15. Check-out: The process of leaving the hotel and settling any outstanding charges.

16. Valet Parking: A parking service in which a hotel employee parks and retrieves guests' vehicles for them.

17. House Count: The total number of guests staying at a hotel at a specific time.

18. Rack Rate: The published room rate for a hotel room, often the highest available rate.

19. All-Inclusive: A type of resort or package that includes all meals, drinks, and activities in the price of the room.

20. Hotel Chain: A group of hotels that operate under the same brand name and management, often with standardized amenities and services.

In conclusion, understanding the terminology of the hotel industry is essential for anyone working or investing in the industry. This glossary provides an overview of some of the most commonly used terms, but it is by no means exhaustive. As the hotel industry continues to evolve, new terms and concepts will continue to emerge.

• Resources for Further Reading and Study

If you are interested in learning more about the hotel industry, here are some resources for further reading and study:

1. Books - There are many books available on the hotel industry that cover a wide range of topics, from hotel management and operations to marketing and revenue management. Some popular titles include "Hotel Management and Operations" by Michael J. O'Fallon and Denney G. Rutherford, "Hotel Front Office Management" by James A. Bardi, and "Marketing in Hospitality" by Ronald A. Nykiel.

2. Trade Associations - There are a number of trade associations in the hotel industry that offer resources and networking opportunities for professionals in the industry. These include the American Hotel & Lodging Association, the International Association of Hospitality Accountants, and the Hospitality Sales and Marketing Association International.

3. Industry Publications - There are many publications that cover news and trends in the hotel industry. Some popular publications

include Hotel Business, Lodging Magazine, and Hospitality Technology.

4. Conferences and Events - Attending industry conferences and events can be a great way to learn about new trends and network with other professionals in the industry. Some popular events include the Hospitality Industry Technology Exposition & Conference (HITEC), the Hotel Experience (HX), and the International Hotel Investment Forum (IHIF).

5. Online Courses and Certifications - There are many online courses and certifications available that cover various aspects of the hotel industry, such as revenue management, marketing, and hospitality management. Some popular providers include the American Hotel & Lodging Educational Institute, Cornell University's School of Hotel Administration, and the Hospitality Sales and Marketing Association International.

In conclusion, the hotel industry is a complex and dynamic industry that offers many opportunities for learning and growth. Whether you are a student, a professional, or an investor, there are many resources available to help you learn about the industry and stay up-to-date on the latest trends and developments.

Printed in Poland
by Amazon Fulfillment
Poland Sp. z o.o., Wrocław
02 October 2023

5dc22981-cb7c-4900-b1d0-18cbc2f795a2R01